BRIAN'S

JOURNEY

THROUGH

GENESIS

BRIAN'S JOURNEY THROUGH GENESIS

Volume 1

The Creation Story

By

BOB LANKFORD

ILLUSTRATIONS BY

RICHIE WILLIAMS

INTRODUCTION

Brian wants to learn more about the Bible. So, why not get your Bible and go along with Brian on his journey through the Bible. These books describing the Bible are in short-story form, using Scripture verses so that you can follow along with Brian, as he takes his journey through the books of the Bible.

You can buy one book at a time and collect all of them or just the ones you want. However, if you start now and collect the whole set, you will be able to solve the puzzle in the last issue.

Brian begins his journey in the book of Genesis with the story of the creation. Illustrations have been provided to help you see what God is teaching Brian on his journey. Also, throughout the book, you will find some word puzzles to complete along the way.

Every 4 to 6 weeks, or at least every other month, a new book will be published so that you can plan your purchases to complete your set. Start your collection now. Read and enjoy!

GENESIS

The Creation

The first set of stories come from the first book in the Bible. That book is called **Genesis**. So, what does the word genesis mean? Well, I am glad you asked, Brian. Genesis means origin, or beginnings—to come into being. The very first verse of the first chapter in Genesis says:

> *"In the beginning God*
> *created the heavens and the earth"*
> (Genesis 1:1).

There was no earth or sky or light. Then, verse 2 says:

*"The earth was formless
and void, and darkness was over
the surface of the deep, and the
Spirit of God was moving over
the surface of the waters"*
(Genesis 1:2).

So, in the very beginning of the world, there was nothing—absolutely nothing! Verse 2 tells us the earth was formless. In other words, the earth was not even formed yet. And since there was no earth and no light, the Spirit of God was the only existence. There was only darkness all around the universe.

Brian, have you ever been in a room late at night where there were no windows or light and you could not even see the nose on your face, or your hand if you put it in front of your eyes? Now, that is what we call dark!

So, God decided to create or bring into existence the formation of the universe. In the first six days, God put everything into existence. God saw that everything he created or brought into existence was good. So, Brian, what do you think God did on the seventh day?

Are you ready to go on that journey? Open your Bible to the first book of Genesis and the first chapter and see what happened. We have already talked about the first two verses.

Now, we will look at these seven days, one day at a time, and we will see what God did on that last day.

Day One

In verse 3, which is day one, God said:

"Let there be light'; and there was light" (Genesis 1:3).

God simply spoke the words *"let there be light"*, and what do you think happened? As soon as he said, *"let there be light,"* there was light all over the universe. This is amazing! God just said the word and it happened. Imagine that! God has the power to just say the words and things happened.

Verse 4 goes on to say:

*"God saw that the light
was good; and God separated the
light from the darkness"*
(Genesis 1:4).

When you are in a room at night and you turn the light switch on, what happens? Suddenly, you have light, and you can now see all around you. That is exactly what God did, only he did not flip a switch. He just spoke the word and there was light.

God was happy with his creation of light so in verse 5 he said:

*"God called the light day,
and the darkness he called night.
And there was evening and there*

was morning, one day" (Genesis 1:5).

Darkness and Light

So, all this is what happened on Day One! Out of nothing God created or brought into existence light and darkness, and he called the light "Day" and the darkness "Night." Now that is amazing!

Unscramble the words to fill in the blanks.

On the first day, God created

G I L T H

— — — — — .

God saw that it was good, and he separated it

or divided it from the

N D K A E S R S

— — — — — — — — .

A Y D

He then called one __ __ __ and

G N H T I

the other one __ __ __ __ __ .

To create these things God just

K S P E O

__ __ __ __ __ the word.

Day Two

In verse 6, God said:

"Let there be an expanse in the midst of the waters, and let it separate the waters from the waters" (Genesis 1:6).

Wow! What does that mean? In this part of the creation, verse 7 tells us, God created a boundary to separate the air from the sea. He created the sky. There was water underneath the sky and water in the sky. We do not know for sure what the "waters above" were, but it could have been clouds, or it could have

been where God keeps the rain until it
was time to let it fall upon the earth.

Clouds above / Water below

Verses 7 and 8 tells us:

1 "God made the expanse,
and separated the waters which
were below the expanse from the
waters which were above the

expanse, and it was so. God called the expanse heaven. And there was evening and there was morning, a second day." What God was doing here is separating heaven from earth. And this became the second day (Genesis 1:7-8).

On the second day, God created a boundary to separate the waters from

R   I   A

the waters by separating __ __ __ from the waters, and that created the

K   S   Y

__ __ __ . God kept the water in

L   O   D   U   C   S

the sky in the __ __ __ __ __ __

N   I   R   A

until it was time for it to __ __ __ __

L   F   A   L

and he would then let it __ __ __ __ to the ground.

Day Three

Verses 9 and 10 tell us what God said next:

> *"Let the waters below the heavens be gathered into one place and let the dry land appear; and it was so. God called the dry land earth, and the gathering of the waters He called seas; and God saw that it was good"* (Genesis1:9-10).

He continued to say in verses 11 and 12 that the earth sprouted trees with fruit, and vegetation with plants growing vegetables and he saw that it was good. And then God said in verse 13:

"There was evening and there was morning, a third day" (Genesis 1:13).

Earth, sky, sea, and trees

Here you can see that God is forming the earth and all the land and

sea and trees and plants. God was busy
on these days.

On the third day, God caused some

D A L N

dry __ __ __ __ to rise from beneath
the waters and God called the

R T E H A

dry ground __ __ __ __ __ . And

E S E T R

from it sprouted __ __ __ __ __ with

U R I F T

__ __ __ __ __ and there were

L P N A S T

__ __ __ __ __ __ growing
vegetables and God saw that it was

O G D O

__ __ __ __ .

Day Four

Now, in verses 14 through 19, God said to let there be lights in the sky and to separate the day from night and let them be for signs and seasons and days and years. The lights were to light up the earth. And when God said that, it happened. God just kept speaking the words, and everything that he said came into existence. That is amazing!

God made two great lights to give light to the earth—a brighter light to brighten the day and a dim light to give a dimmer light at night. Do you know what those lights are? Of course, you do; the sun in the daytime and the moon and stars in the nighttime. God saw that all this too was good and then there was evening and there was morning, the fourth day.

Moon and stars and the Sun

On the fourth day, God created lights to be in the sky to separate the day from the night.

G S N I S

They were to be for __ __ __ __ __ and

Y S D A

for seasons and for __ __ __ __ and

R E Y S A

__ __ __ __ __ .

G I L T H

The lights were to __ __ __ __ __ up the

R T E H A   M D I

__ __ __ __ __ . The __ __ __ lights were

O M O N   T S A S R

the __ __ __ __ and __ __ __ __ __ . The

U S N

bright one was the __ __ __ .

Day Five

"Then God said,

"Let the waters teem with

swarms of living creatures, and let

birds fly above the earth in the

open expanse of the heavens.

God created the

great sea monsters and every living

creature that moves, with which

the waters swarmed after their

kind, and every winged bird after

its kind; and God saw that it was

good (Genesis 1:20-21).*"*

In verses 20 through 21, God then
created or brought into existence,

swarms of living creatures with birds and fish, and he saw that it was good. He blessed them and told them to multiply. That means he wanted them to produce little birds and fish just like them.

Birds and Fish

On this fifth day, God created the

D I R B S   H I F S

__ __ __ __ __ **and** __ __ __ __ .

And he told them to go out and multiply,
which means to have lots of what?

S A B E I B

__ __ __ __ __ __ .

Day Six

On this last day of God's creation, he decided it was time to create or bring into existence animals and man.

Animals and Man

God was so happy and pleased with what he had done that he said let us make man in our image. Why is he saying, "our image?" This is what makes man's creation different from the animals. Man was made in the likeness of God's image because man is an intelligent or smart being. Man was made with a free will and a moral nature. That means that man was given the ability to make choices. That ability causes man to understand what is right and what is wrong.

If you notice in the beginning, God was not alone. Also present was the Holy Spirit and his Son Jesus. So, he needed to make man in their image. When he did that, he was pleased and there was evening and there was morning, the sixth day.

So, on this sixth day, God decided
it was time to create or bring into

M I N   A L   A   S

existence __ __ __ __ __ __ __ and,
most important of all, he wanted to
create a human and he called it what? He

N   M   A

called it __ __ __ . God created him in

U   R   O

his who's image? Yes, it said __ __ __
image. And who was he referring to?
D   G   O   O   L   H   Y

__ __ __ , the __ __ __ __
T   S   I   P   I   R

__ __ __ __ __ __ and
S   U   J   E   S

__ __ __ __ __ .

Day Seven

"Thus the heavens and the earth were completed, and all their hosts.

By the seventh day God completed His work which He had done, and He rested on the seventh day from all His work which He had done.

Then God blessed the seventh day and sanctified it, because in it He rested from all His work which God had created and made (Genesis 2:1-3)."

The Bible now tells us in Genesis 2:1-3 that everything God created or brought into existence was completed and God was very happy with his creation. On this seventh day, God decided to rest from all the work which he had done. So, God blessed this day and called it holy.

What do you think was the one thing God loved most about his work of creation? The one thing God loved most of all his creation was us, the people. That is still true to this day. He created us to have a relationship with him.

This seventh day was called the Sabbath day. Sabbath means holy and God designed it to be a day of rest and for worship. That is why one of the Ten Commandments given by God says to remember the Sabbath day and keep it holy.

Now that was the story of how everything, including you and me, came into being. And all God had to do was just what? He just had to speak the word, and it all happened.

See you in the next book, Brian!

ABOUT THE AUTHOR

Bob Lankford is a retired Baptist pastor who entered ministry late in life, at the age of thirty-seven. He worked in banking and finance before moving into the manufacturing field, promoting up to supervisory ranks for several years. Ministry was the furthest thing from his mind, when the Lord finally began to work in his life, eventually calling him into full-time gospel ministry.

Bob and his wife Deanna and two children, Stephanie and Brian packed up everything they had, sold their house, and moved to Ft. Worth, TX where he would attend Southwestern Baptist Theological Seminary, to pursue an Associate of Divinity degree in 1984.

After pastoring for many years, he eventually retired and moved back to Texas. He and Deanna ended up in Denison, Texas near Lake Texoma where they bought a home and settled down.

God laid on Bob's heart to write. He wrote daily devotions and was published in David C. Cook's publication of *Devotions* magazine.

Bob is the leader of Texoma Christian Writers Group which has only just begun. You can keep up with Bob's blogs at his author's website www.boblankford.com. You can sign up for his monthly newsletter at his site as well.

Here Bob begins his newest venture with Brian's Journey Through the Bible, beginning with the book of Genesis and starting with the creation story, followed by several more stories to be published individually.